Bug Patrol

LOOKING FOR SPIDERS

Written by

EMILIE DUFRESNE

KidHaven
PUBLISHING

Published in 2023 by KidHaven Publishing,
an Imprint of Greenhaven Publishing, LLC
29 East 21st Street
New York, NY 10010

Edited by:
Madeline Tyler

Designed by:
Brandon Mattless

Cataloging-in-Publication Data

Names: Dufresne, Emilie.
Title: Looking for spiders / Emilie Dufresne.
Description: New York : KidHaven Publishing, 2023. | Series: Bug patrol |
Includes glossary and index.
Identifiers: ISBN 9781534541252 (pbk.) | ISBN 9781534541276 (library bound)
| ISBN 9781534541269 (6 pack) | ISBN 9781534541283 (ebook)
Subjects: LCSH: Spiders--Juvenile literature.
Classification: LCC QL458.4 D84 2023 | DDC 595.4'4--dc23

Manufactured in the United States of America

CPSIA compliance information: Batch #CSKH23: For further information contact Greenhaven Publishing LLC, New York, New York at 1-844-317-7404.

Please visit our website, www.greenhavenpublishing.com.
For a free color catalog of all our high-quality books,
call toll free 1-844-317-7404 or fax 1-844-317-7405.

Photo Credits

All images are courtesy of Shutterstock.com, unless otherwise specified. With thanks to Getty Images, Thinkstock Photo and iStockphoto.
Front Cover – Paladin12, Gluiki, Rudmer Zwerver, Vova Shevchuk. Recurring Images – Gluiki, Natee Photo, Paladin12, photka. 4–5 – ieuan, Per-Boge, zhukovvvlad. 6–7 – Alexey Chernitevich, Anatoliy Sadovskiy, Ivan Semenovych, Karkas, kdshutterman, Sevendayimages. 8–9 – Luis Felipe Zagatto, Zeren Z. 10–11 – aaltair, HHelene, Marek Velechovsky, MF Photo. 12–13 – Eric Isselee, papkin, ShaunWilkinson, TTstudio, veronchick_84. 14–15 – lucag_g, Moisieiev Igor, Sandra Standbridge. 16–17 – Pan Xunbin, Sopha Changaroon, tome213. 18–19 – Cornel Constantin, Henrik Larsson, Miles Boyer. 20–21 – Andrey_Kuzmin, NaturePixel, Zety Akhzar, Jürgen Otto.

CONTENTS

Words that look like **this** can be found in the glossary on page 24.

GO OUTSIDE!

It is time to go outside to look for creatures!

Where will you go?

Keep an eye out. Creatures can live in very small spaces!

BE READY!

Make sure you are ready to explore. You will need:

A coat

A magnifying glass

A drink

A snack

BE KIND!

Do not touch or move any animals you find. Do not get too close.

Some spiders can be dangerous. Do not touch spiders you find.

WHAT IS A SPIDER?

Spiders live all over the world. They are a type of **arachnid**. They have eight legs.

Some spiders are small, and some are big.

Many spiders make webs to catch their **prey**. There are different types of spider webs.

Whenever you see a hand, place your hand on the page to see how big the spider is.

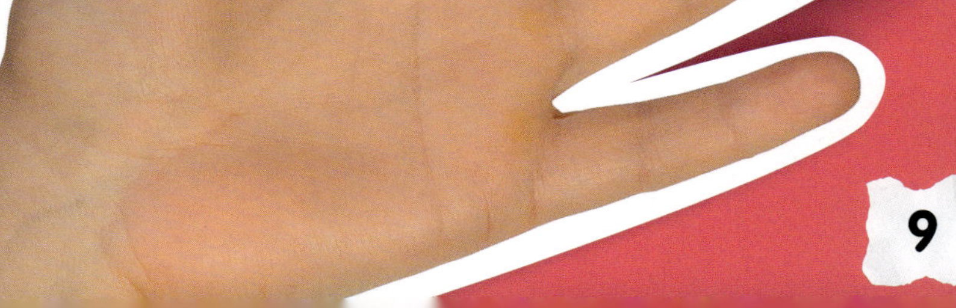

LADYBIRD SPIDER

Male ladybird spiders are bright red with black spots. They look a bit like ladybugs!

Actual size

Place your hand here

Ladybug

Ladybird spiders can be hard to spot because they live in **burrows** underground.

Female ladybird spiders are mostly black.

GARDEN SPIDER

Actual size

Garden spiders can be found in gardens. Their webs have a spiral shape in them.

Place your hand here

Spiral shape

Garden spiders are easy to spot. They have a white cross shape on them.

Female garden spiders are bigger and rounder than male garden spiders.

WASP SPIDER

Female wasp spider

Female wasp spiders have yellow and black stripes. They look a bit like wasps.

Actual size

Place your hand here

They **weave** their webs with a zigzag pattern down the middle.

SPINY ORB-WEAVER SPIDER

Spiny orb-weaver spiders have spines on them. This keeps them safe from **predators**.

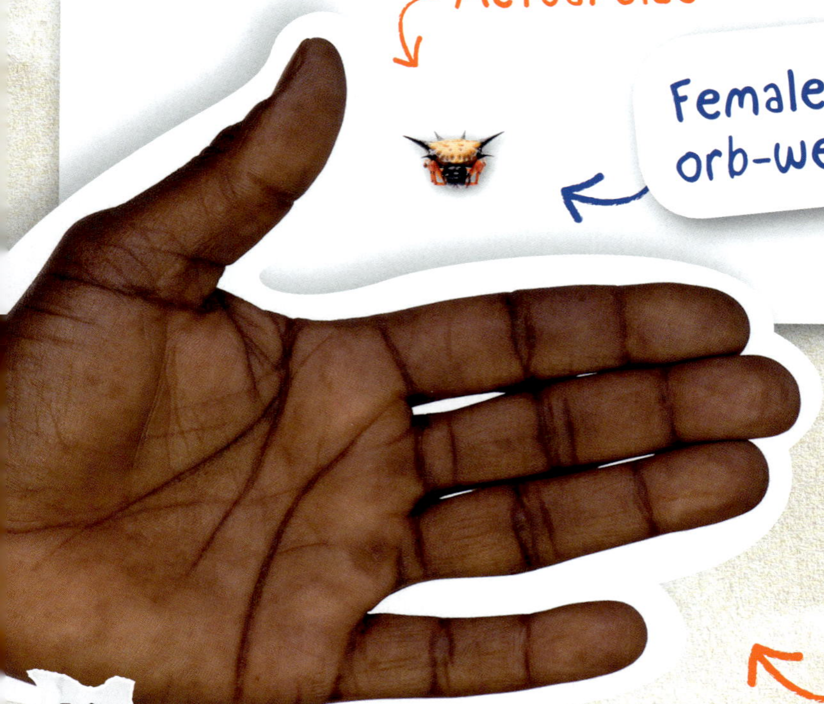

Female spiny orb-weaver spider

Spiny orb-weaver spiders can be different colors. They can also have different spines.

How many spines can you count?

WOLF SPIDER

Wolf spiders can sometimes be found sunbathing in warm places.

Actual size

Place your hand here

Female wolf spiders carry their babies on their backs for a few days after they hatch.

Baby spiders are called spiderlings.

PEACOCK SPIDER

Male peacock spiders can be very colorful. They look like a rainbow!

Actual size

How many colors can you see?

Place your hand here

Male peacock spiders are good dancers! They dance to attract a mate, and make a fan like a peacock's tail.

Peacock spider

Peacock fan

SPIDER PATROL

We've learned about super spiders around the world. What kinds of spiders live near you? Time to explore!

Ladybird spider

Garden Spider

Wasp spider

Spiny orb-weaver spider

Wolf spider

Peackock spider

It's time to go... looking for spiders!

GLOSSARY

arachnid a type of animal that has eight legs, such as spiders and scorpions

burrows underground tunnels that animals live in

predators animals that eat other animals for food

prey animals that are eaten by other animals for food

weave tying threads together in a special way

INDEX